" *On Trampolining* is a jewel of an essay, where like the most gifted artisan, Rebecca Perry reconstructs shattered pieces of a life spent loftily, into a fragile work of quivering wonder, of flesh and bone and sparkling clarity. I read it swiftly, holding my breath the whole way through."

—Inua Ellams

"A tremendous, compelling read. It sheds light on a sport I know nothing about, and the pressures it takes to be even very, very good at something, let alone close to the best in the world."

—Rishi Dastidar

ON TRAMPOLINING

© Rebecca Perry, 2023

Design and illustration by Patrick Fisher of Frontwards Design
Photograph of Rebecca Perry by Robin Christian

ISBN: 978-1-7396160-1-4

First published in the UK in 2023 by Makina Books
makinabooks.com

Printed in the UK by Pureprint Group

Earlier versions of this work have been previously published in
Pain journal (2019) and *Stone Fruit* (Bloodaxe Books, 2021).

ON TRAMPOLINING

REBECCA PERRY

*

As a child, I had a large, hardback book of stories which, for a while, I read nightly. The cover was glossy, yellow, and intricately illustrated.

One story, whose exact beginning escapes me, ended with a beast and a young girl walking for miles through the wilderness.

The beast, to make the way safe for them, goes ahead to vanquish an enemy in a duel. The young girl is instructed to wait for him on a fallen tree trunk. She is not to move in any way, not even to blink, until he returns to her.

He leaves, and she obeys.

Days pass. The beast wins his victory and the sky flashes. In excitement, knowing what this means, without even feeling it, her foot twitches, barely at all.

That very second the girl turns to stone. The girl as well as the beast, far away, and all the land between them. The tree she sits on, and the grass where her feet rest, every blade. The trees and the fruit that hangs from them, fruit that was ripe and ready to be taken, which she had resisted despite the heat and the thirst and the days of waiting, all now irreversibly set in place, sucked of colour, never to feed insect, bird or passer-by.

She had failed in so inconceivably small a way. She had failed utterly.

W hen I was a trampolinist I had never felt like my movements were really taken on by my body.

It was more like my mind forced the movements into being, rather than them happening in a way that felt instinctive or magical or inevitable.

I still imagine that a really gifted athlete becomes their movements, as if the muscles absorb them – no divisions or edges – the brain an ice cube melting into the body.

The brain is like a horse. You love the horse. The horse's nose is so soft but it will throw you off into a shallow stream and make you eat mud.

A gifted athlete is able to tame their brain in such a way that their thoughts become like water, by which I mean blood, running into every corner, but still under command.

My mind would throw me backwards instead of forwards, trick me to land on my neck.

I was not a gifted athlete. I knew it.

I persisted.

*

The pupil is mistaken about what he thinks he sees. A common example of this is experienced at the railway station, when the train at the next platform starts to move and you feel that your train is moving. The pupil looks for visual clues and opens out from the somersault on seeing the white ceiling in mistake for the white bed.
—*Trampolining for Coaches and Performers* by Rob Walker

The beginning. My mum met Neece at NCT class, they had their first children – my brother and James – a month apart, their second children – me and Scott – two years later, 10 days apart.

Rob – James and Scott's dad – took up a voluntary position as a trampolining coach at a local leisure centre when I was three, at my mum's suggestion. We all went along on Saturday afternoons.

I have only two memories of my childhood that aren't of, or adjacent to, trampolining and competing. Unzipping tracksuits – stretching – saluting – lying on mesh and looking up at the ceiling – sitting on benches – back straight – in hall after hall – waiting my turn – training that evening – a competition that weekend. I have only two memories before this all began, is my belief, was my belief.

The first, I am being pushed through the hallway of our house in a buggy, towards the front door. The bright light coming through the wavy glass of the front door panels tells me it is daytime. Spring or summer.

The second, I am sitting on the floor of the front room in my maternal grandparents' house. Leaning left onto a pouffe, eating mint choc chip ice cream from a white bowl. The curtains are drawn. Daytime. Strips of light haunting the edges of the fabric in dislocated rectangles. Cigarette smoke turning the air milky. We – being me, my mum, dad and brother, and my nan and grandad – watched a documentary about sea life. The film on the screen was underwater, quite dark blue, and a large silver fish, maybe two, swam by.

Many people believe they have a memory of being in their

buggy, or their cot. Almost certainly they don't, and therefore almost certainly I don't.

Being as my grandparents both died, six months apart, when I was three, and studies suggest that memories formed at that age are more likely than not to be false, I have to assume that this never happened. Or it happened partially, in scattered components, or in a dream. When I recall the memory I feel that I felt I was sitting inside a protective box, like an aquarium, and the dark of the room with its misty air was also the dark of the fish's habitat. I ate my ice cream so neatly.

My mum has verified that my brother and I were taken to Neece and Rob's to be looked after when her mum was very close to death, and I'm sure I remember this. We stood at the entrance to the porch, which was too small to stand inside. I probably looked at the fish in the little, dark pond in their front garden, as I always did while we waited. Neece opened the door and ushered us in, touching my shoulder. I have allowed one of my implausible memories to be true and have settled on this one.

A fundamental part of successful trampolining is landing on the central red cross every time your feet hit the mesh, which is called the bed.

In a single routine you land ten moves.

A move is whatever formal shape or rotation you can achieve in the space between taking off and landing again.

Colloquially, to trampoline is to 'bounce'.

Journeying away from the red cross, the sweet spot where the bed is at its softest, results to some lesser or greater degree in an uneven landing. An uneven landing means a less stable return jump, which means less height, a more rushed routine, a frantic spiral.

And so, landing on the red cross results in greater height in the return jump. Greater height means more time in the air. More time means that moves can be completed calmly, fluidly and safely, with poise and style. A clean routine.

More time also means more complex moves can be introduced – a double somersault instead of one, a double twist instead of single.

Marks are given for 'time of flight', the amount of time a competitor spends in the air, and deducted for venturing outside of the red box which surrounds the central cross. I was afraid of the red cross, its capacity to catapult you into a realm of pure possibility.

At each competition, every performer must complete two routines. First, a set, or compulsory, routine, which is assigned according to your grade and age. This routine is performed by every competitor in your category – a means of direct comparison. The compulsory routine is tailored to the skill level of the group and it is expected that it will be executed perfectly. Second, a voluntary routine, or 'vol', comprised of the 10 moves which will best demonstrate your skill and ability. A riskier display, usually considerably more difficult, a chance for you to show what you're made of.

—

It is customary at competitions for spectators to fall silent when a competitor salutes the judges and begins the first jumps of a routine. The quiet is punctuated by the springs creaking their extension when contact is made with the bed, and the tap of the rubber soles of trampolining shoes connecting with the mesh. A light tap. A very clean sound.

—

A leotard is like a second skin. Black and green lycra. Red, white and navy velour. A fluorescent baby pink two-piece. Purple velvet with a swirling constellation on the chest made of silver beads. Matching scrunchies. A second skin wriggled into and peeled off. For girls, full-length sleeves for competitions. For boys, no sleeves but a pair of whites – jodhpur-style trousers with an elastic strip that runs under the heel to keep them in place.

—

My hair was French plaited before each competition. Neat, tight, no strays, set to solidity with hairspray. The pull at the temples was a grounding in the body, a fixing.

—

If you had an accident when performing a certain move, you had to do that move again immediately, before the fear set in. Jump back on the horse.

—

It was common for athletes to 'lose' moves, meaning that the knowledge of how to conduct it was wiped from the memory seemingly overnight. Often the move was a simple one, learned many years earlier and conducted thousands of times. One day you would mount the bed and attempt the move either as a warm up, without even thinking ahead to it, and realise in the preceding jumps that it wasn't going to be possible. Other times you would mentally think through a routine in advance of carrying it out only to reach a precipice, no road ahead.

Did the brain get full? Was it sending a capacity warning?

Then would begin the process of relearning the move. Word circulating around the club that you had lost it. Going back to the basics of breaking the move into its component parts - rotations and twists – executing it with no natural instinct, the feeling of it, the familiarity of it, all gone.

—

There are many terms for the act of failing to complete a full routine in competition. Failure can look like:

- Landing on the blue mat at either end of the bed
- Clipping the blue perimeter with a heel
- Under-or-over- rotation of a move
- Falling from the bed entirely

Messing up. Bombing. Choking. Crashing out.

In many other sports, there typically exists some hope of redemption. You can win the ball back, play better on the next point, hop back on the beam. Failure in trampolining is more final. When the routine has been interrupted, you do not begin again or pick up where you left off.

You salute, dismount.

There are two VHS tapes of me performing full routines. In the first I am four years old. I wear our black and green club leotard and my hair is plaited, slapping down on my upper back each time I land. I perform what was then, in 1989, the classic Grade D beginner routine.

- Full twist
- Straddle
- Seat drop
- Half twist to seat drop
- Half twist to feet
- Pike jump
- Back drop
- Half twist to feet
- Tuck jump
- Front somersault

It is an almost perfect display until a whipped final move propels me a metre or so forward. The video is taken at standing height a few metres from the trampoline, most likely by Rob. My mum and dad would have been close by and my brother would have been in his leotard and whites, ready to compete later as we progressed through the age groups. My parents, out of shot but certainly there, only metres away, were younger than I am now.

The front somersault is the first and easiest somersault new trampolinists learn. A simple journey, heels over head, feet to feet. To start the learning process, the coach will offer two-handed support, placing one hand on the shoulder closest to them, and the other on your hip, perhaps holding the elasticated waist of your shorts or joggers. You take small, tentative jumps, and the coach jumps alongside you, keeping time. Another person will be ready to the side of the bed with a crash mat to soften your landing. On your first try you will, inevitably, either over-rotate and need to be halted mid-air, or under-rotate and need to be flipped the rest of the way by the coach.

I don't remember learning my first somersault. I accumulated them without thinking. I was in the air, upside down, as I was at school, in the bath, eating dinner with my family.

*

I kept trying to locate the story in the yellow book. I scoured the internet, adding new details to search terms when something specific – the sky turned red when it flashed? They had escaped from a castle? – occurred to me. I changed details I wasn't sure of – perhaps the beast was actually a boar, maybe the girl was not a child at all but a young woman fleeing an unwanted marriage. It could even be that the sky didn't flash at all, but a loud crack, like thunder, alerted her to the victory. But I knew she waited for days, her foot twitched, and she turned to stone.

Ancient literature is littered with petrification – people cursed to solidity by beasts and gods for their vanity, or their pride or greed. Medusa was driven by pure hatred of mortal men, Poseidon by revenge, fixing a whole ship and its crew to the bed of the ocean. Hermes by the sting of betrayal.

In more recent fairy tales, people tend to be turned to stone for failing to obey a simple command, and await return to human form at the hands of a less foolish hero. But the girl's command was not simple, and no one was coming to save her.

Club competitions came first – friendly, informal, a chance for people to test out new routines. Our parents would compete too, without seriousness, and the children would be amused by their efforts. I enjoyed these internal competitions. Because the space, the beds, the people, were familiar? Because there was nothing really to be lost in the event of failure? Because most of my friends at the club weren't as good as me?

Medals and trophies started to fill the cubby under the stairs. I often won silver or bronze and told myself I preferred those colours to gold, which was crass and ugly and for show-offs. As I began to win competitions more regularly I wonder if this position changed. I don't remember.

I liked the safety of a routine I knew well, that didn't challenge me, luxuriating in the certainty of success. I liked not being afraid. I liked the weight of a medal on a ribbon hanging around my neck. I liked leotards and their dynamic patterns, often clashing colourways, the way their closeness brought with it an enhanced awareness of the contours of your body – every inch of your torso, chest and arms. I liked making a move my own with a small flourish, a placement of an arm. I liked, for one split second at the top of a jump, the feeling of floating.

*

There are a range of support methods available to coaches when teaching a new move. Support methods ensure that, as much as possible, an athlete isn't harmed during the learning process.

Support by the hands

Only suitable for moves which require little height and minimal twisting, in order that the coach can keep one hand or two on the trampolinist at all times. Mostly used for a single front or back somersault. I was never uncomfortable being supported in this way, and there is something immediate and reassuring about the proximity of another body, their breath in your ear as they count you in – 'ready, one, two…' – but I always preferred the moment I could break free in the air, held only by the pinch of their thumb and forefinger, like the moment you break away from a hug and can look the other person in the eye.

Crash mat

A soft blue mat, much like a mattress, which is pushed onto the trampoline to break the fall of the trampolinist. The benefits are twofold: first, an awkward or potentially dangerous landing is softened, the impact and capacity for grazing your skin on the rough bed is lessened; second, the mat kills the rebound, so a landing at an angle will not propel the trampolinist off the trampoline and into the wall or to the floor. The crash mat was a huge comfort but, with its lack of repercussions, could get you into bad habits.

Kipping and killing

Less widely used, kipping is the act of gifting artificial height by jumping or pressing down into the bed before a trampolinist lands a jump. Caught in the rebound, they are pinged into the air with their own force and the additional force of the kipper. While extra height is beneficial for completing more somersaults or twists, the bounce itself is often uncontrolled. Killing is essentially the opposite of kipping, with a coach jumping or pressing down into the bed at the point of landing, absorbing the give of the netting and ensuring a landing has no dangerous return jump. Kipping was mostly used as part of a 10 minute playing around session at the end of training. I liked the sensation of my body being possessed by an energy totally outside of my own. But it also felt risky, uncontrollable.

The rig

As the complexity (and therefore associated risk) of new moves increased, we would often resort to using the rig for the initial phase of learning. For all intents and purposes a simple harness assembled above a trampoline, the rig also resembles a chastity belt, and allows an athlete to be held aloft at the end of a rope. A coach would operate the rope, allowing slack for the descent and pulling down on the rope in the ascent. Ultimately, the rope can be tightened at any moment, suspending you in the air before you have the chance to land dangerously. The idea of the rig is that you get used to the sensation of a move. You experiment with the timing of twists and extension without fear of injury. It requires a great deal of trust on the part of the trampolinist, in much the same way as a rock climber must rely on the belayer below them, holding the ropes. Before I began jumping I would often say to Rob, 'Are you paying attention? Are you sure you're ready? Do you promise?'

*

I also attended gymnastics classes until my parents were given an ultimatum by the coach there: trampolining or gymnastics, one or the other. It was up to me.

The gymnastics coaches sometimes applied pressure to force our bodies into certain positions. I can't remember a single one of their names or faces. We spent so much time on the ground, stretching through pain into pikes and splits. Cheek to the floor, forehead to the floor.

I trained with slightly older girls who seemed cold and distant. The atmosphere was sharp. I remember it being quiet, or feeling quiet, and whispers.

I once vomited when we did backflip after backflip on the long blue strip mat. An older girl was told to take me down to the toilets to clean me up. When we were alone, she demanded to know why I hadn't told anyone if I knew I was going to be sick. I told her I hadn't known.

Once, a fellow gymnast lost grip on the bars and flew into the corner, landing on a collection of wooden vaulting horses. We were immediately moved to a different part of the gymnasium.

There was a girl called Leah. We were friends. I was jealous of her name.

I found the beam and the bars aggressive in their solidity – restrictive in their pinning of you to an object. Things to slip and fall from. Floor gymnastics made me feel too visible – every bone in a foot flexing to keep balance observable by the judges and audience. No mystery, no escape. A trampoline was a partner, allowing itself to be used, encouraging freedom.

The trampolining coaches had never posed an ultimatum. I loved my friends there, our easiness, the loudness of the hall mid-session, the rhythm of the springs.

I chose air over earth.

*

Another story in the yellow book involves two boys – I think brothers – whose job is to fix the shoes of the neighbourhood.

Instead of fixing the shoes, at the end of each day they walk to the precipice of their high-up garden and throw them into the night. The shoes would fly back to them the next morning, fixed and shining and looking better than new.

I remember nothing else besides an illustration of a mountain of shoes building up and the boys thinking their trick (whatever it was) beyond comeuppance. It was not.

The details of this story have not helped me to locate the stone girl.

*

Whenever a trampoline is in use, both during practice and competition, 'spotters' must stand guard at the edge. The job of a spotter is to watch the athlete closely, anticipate danger and, if necessary, block the body if it comes perilously close to the perimeter of the trampoline. We would take turns to spot during training, fidgeting at the corners of the bed. I must have spent hundreds of hours watching James and Scott, my neck tipped back, understanding without even knowing it when their brain or body was about to fail them.

When my brother and I shared a room, we had two goldfish in a rectangular tank on top of the chest of drawers. The larger fish was his. The smaller fish was mine. They had their little cube and we had ours. We fed them the customary multi-coloured flakes from a tub and held the tips of our fingers just below the surface of the water for them to mistake for food. I was grateful for the sound of the filter at night, and the low blue glow of the tank's light. Always seeking my brother's outline underneath his duvet when I couldn't sleep.

I sometimes slept badly as a child – scared of the dark and whatever could be hiding in cupboards and under the bed. Scared of the quiet of it, the stillness, as if life had stopped.

There is a famous anecdote in my family: having shared a bedroom with my brother for seven years, I was finally due to move into my own room down the hall. On the evening of the move, my brother told me that ghosts of Victorian people like to hide in cupboards and jump out in the night, which is exactly what he did, albeit as a living nine-year-old boy with a toothbrush in his mouth, before the lights had even been turned out.

My brother took swimming lessons on Saturday mornings, before my training in the afternoon at the same leisure centre. I would eat a sandwich from its foil wrapper and watch him move through the water. He had stopped trampolining at Grade D, as Scott, James and I moved upwards through the grades. He preferred gadgets and lights and building things. At one session, my brother was being supported by Rob to complete his first back somersault. The point at which he was due to take off coincided with James kicking a football into a wall-mounted goal post in the hall. He jumped onto the goal, whose frame was metal, and pulled it from the wall on top of himself. He lay there on the ground, with the top of the goal on his temple, eyes open and unfocused. He looked dead. Rob jumped from the bed leaving my brother in mid-air, embarking on this new move suddenly without support. That was the end of it for him.

I had not enjoyed learning to swim in the huge, dark municipal pool closest to our house. The deep end seemed cold and bottomless. The water felt heavy on my body, as if it was pushing me down at the shoulders – too dense, my limbs too slow.

Our friend from trampolining lived in a house with an aviary and a wall-sized fish tank, two chinchillas who slept in a cage by the front door, and many stick insects, though the house itself was relatively small. Among the many wonders of the aquarium were two kissing gourami who could swim barely ten seconds without stopping to peck one another, their lips flattening suddenly into perfect circles, like two tiny white plates.

If a person failed to display adequate core strength when trampolining, they would bend slightly in the middle, with their legs lagging behind the rest of their body. This was particularly obvious when performing straight moves, where the expectation is that the body be stiff as a board from top to toe, presenting a perfectly straight line. Like a pin. Where a person failed in this they were said to be flapping about like a fish. Points would be deducted for poor form.

When I left behind the pursuit of gymnastics, I remember that I missed only the chalking of hands before mounting the bar or horse.

I think it was more than simply missing the feeling of the powder, softer than talc, and the creak of your hand pushing down into the barrel.

More likely it was the fact that the chalk was being relied upon for grip.

When something is being relied upon it can feasibly malfunction and any failure cannot be your fault alone.

*

My body was nothing to me at this time. It was neither comfortable nor uncomfortable. It just was. It helped me with my gymnastics career and it burned when the skin rubbed off my palms from too much time on the uneven bars and it throbbed when I twisted my ankle but other than that I didn't think about it very much at all.
—My Body Keeps Your Secrets, Lucia Osborne-Crowley

I never felt worn out or tired.

Sometimes, after an hour and a half or so of training, I might start to make mistakes or lose height and the coach would say, 'We'll stop now – you're tired.'

I had no real concept of the feeling – I never noticed that my body was struggling. Other than injuries it never ached, my muscles never complained. I hardly recall sweating.

Even panting from exertion felt almost neutral – no discomfort.

I think about this sometimes when I am out of breath, arms aching, doing backstroke in the pool – how easy it was in the beginning, how my body did whatever I asked of it.

After some years of solo trampolining, I was paired with a partner for synchronised competition. Sophie. We were well matched – both unspectacular, but fairly consistent. Our training was harmonious and forgettable. She had thick brown hair. I have no memory of who made the approach, or who decided we would work together, but one day there she was in my life, on the next trampoline. A different round of competitions, a different set of leotards.

Scott and I had competed as a mixed pair, informally, at club level. I had loved that. I knew he would never care if I messed up, and I felt the same. We had spent the entirety of our lives in each other's company. He told me recently that he had just enjoyed the act of trampolining, that he can never really remember worrying about it. His most vivid memory is of one of the older children at the club pulling out four of his teeth which were slightly loose, but not ready to be separated from his body.

*

In synchronised trampolining, it must appear as if you are jumping next to a mirror, not two people, but one, reflecting an alternate body. The more you and your partner are physically alike, the better. If your hair is the same colour and length, you are of similar weights and heights, perfect.

*

In the glitter on the floor of the toilet cubicle, two dots are identical. Locate them and place one on your cheek, one on hers.

*

Although synchronicity is measured primarily on a pair landing each move at exactly the same time, and secondarily on each move being a mirror image – the kick out of the tuck at the same time and angle, the presentation of the chest in perfect tandem – if one of the pair is inches taller than the other, the reach of their jump will appear higher to the eye. Messy.

During a synchronised competition you are judged as an individual as well as a pair. One judge, the 'de-sync judge', is watching specifically to record any lack of synchronisation in a routine. Other judges are assigned to each performer, marking your individual display out of 10.

There is a pleasure in falling in line with another body. And in sensing what is to come from it. Bending yours to match, applying force, pulling back, correcting. Controlling every movement so it is both your movement and theirs. Looking straight ahead but only *really* looking at the blur in your peripheral vision, where your twin exists. The pressure, the possibility of failing, doubled, yet also halved by the potential for someone else to fail you. Which would have been fine by me.

We found ourselves, in 1995, at the national finals for synchronised trampolining, competing in the under 11s category. After our final routine, we knelt in front of the black computer monitor with its green neon text and waited for the scores to come in and our position to be calculated. Arms wrapped around each other. We had won. I remember the sheer excitement of it, the surprise. I don't think it had even crossed our minds.

Our leotards were purple – between plum and violet – with flat silver beading in swirls across the chest. I loved to touch the beading with a flat hand, perhaps test out the resistance of a bead with a fingernail.

*

Once, at an away competition, in a place none of us can remember, there was an accident.

In my mum and dad's joint memory, a group of us children were running around inside near the entrance to the hotel. My brother ran into the glass doors by reception, which had no stickers or signs on them to make them visible. My dad thinks the glass broke, my mum isn't sure. They remember the feeling of relief, bordering on disbelief, that he was unharmed. A member of staff, who they took to be the manager, told them not to worry about the damage.

According to my brother, everyone was outside the hotel having a drink apart from the two of us, who had stayed in the hotel room. We decided to race and my brother was winning, which turned into me chasing him. When he turned to see how close I was, he ran into the glass, the side-turn of his face protecting his nose. He recalls that it didn't break properly, but it did crack.

I remember that I chased my brother down some stairs into a hotel foyer. Everyone else was sitting near the bar area having a drink. My brother turned his head to look at me and ran straight into the large sliding door, which cracked all over but remained as one sheet. Then he fell backwards to the floor. Or he bounced back from the glass as if expelled by a spirit.

He spent so many hours of his life in these places because of me. Whole days sitting on stadium seating in halls with no windows, in cars, in other cities, watching me, James and Scott.

*

My heel failed first – I was around ten, seven years into my career. Training probably three times a week at this point: Thursday and Friday evenings, Saturday afternoons. A dullish sharp pain when I landed on the bed that persisted when I walked and ran.

A chiropractor treated my spine by twisting my hip towards him and pushing my shoulder towards the wall. He treated my ankles and shoulders. He didn't explain the relevance of Achilles to my inflamed Achilles tendon which I would later consider a missed opportunity. Why didn't he speak over the crunch of my bones? Why not some attempt at comfort? Perhaps he enjoyed playing the instrument of the human form.

That little room of discomfort. The high table with the paper cover. The clock. The desk. The bone crack.

He asked to treat my neck: problems pass from top to bottom. I said no. I had cricked my neck the year before and couldn't walk for days. Couldn't move at all in the white hot pain. My brother did the same and his lips turned blue. At the next appointment my heel was worse. The chiropractor said he had warned me this would happen. Sometimes I would sit on the edge of the table and he would be behind me, perhaps manipulating my shoulders, and I would freeze with the expectation that he would grip my neck and twist it without warning, catching me off guard.

I recall that I enjoyed the feeling of the ankle support and the pain was bearable. Eventually it faded.

*

When I was around six, training on a Friday night, an older girl landed on the trampoline in a seated position with her legs slightly bent. The impact smashed her face into her knees like a coconut on a countertop. When I went into the toilets she was being held at one elbow by my mum and at the other by Neece.

The girl was facing the mirror – her whole face red with blood and her teeth bright white, framed by the blood she was spitting out and losing down her chin into the sink. Her crying echoed in a flat way, the toilets being in the basement and windowless.

Her face was reflected in the mirrors in front of her and on either side. A multiplicity of red monsters. Her eyes flicked to meet mine in the mirror when I entered. My mum told me, kindly, to leave. The girl had her cheek reconstructed with a metal plate. What is the role of pain in the process of learning?

*

The chiropractor held my foot, cupped in his two hands. My foot in a white sock. He pulled my heel towards him, holding my Achilles tendon between this thumb and forefinger, and applied pressure to the backs of my toes with his palm. Pushing my foot back on itself. The girl in the story twitched her foot. I wonder if it was a twist of the heel or a wiggle of the toes.

He mentioned delayed bruising. Invisible bruising. Tenderness. Tension. I thought of my foot as an apple dropped on the floor, replaced hastily in the bowl, left to develop a patch of mush.

Trampolining, the GP believed, is what caused my hymen to half break then attempt to heal. I went to him and told him there was a lump in my cervix.

The high table with the paper cover.

After he had checked it, back in the consulting room, I couldn't take my eyes off his hands. As I was leaving the surgery, almost at his door, he stopped me and said, *vagina, not cervix*. I felt ashamed by this correcting of my body, that I couldn't even label myself, my fingers on the door handle, and carried my shame out into the world. He had not been particularly gentle or kind.

I was in my early teens and did not believe what he said, instead expecting it to shrink or grow huge and malignant. I would check the progress of the lump in the bath then quickly withdraw my finger. I hated to touch it.

*

In my teens, I began to detest pips inside fruit. Apples and pears were fine, with their reliable, sheltered clusters, as was anything with a large, single stone, such as a plum or mango. But citrus fruits, with their way of concealing the hidden tooth, the lack of predictability of their whereabouts, became something that required inspection.

I would nibble the skin at the seam of the segment, then peel down the segment walls, behold the segment de-robed. I preferred the texture of the compressed vesicles exposed against my tongue. I liked to compress it between my tongue and the roof of my mouth.

When this full stripping of the segment wasn't possible – such as at school – I would hold each segment up to the light to decipher a shadow. If a pip was suspected, I would nibble the seam and pull it open enough to check. If there was one pip inside I would squeeze it out onto something (not my hand) and eat the fruit, first putting the tip of my tongue into the space left by the pip.

If, during the inspection, a segment was revealed to have multiple pips – any more than two – it would have to be discarded along with the offending cluster.

Hymenoptera is the order of insects that includes ants, wasps and bees, from the Greek hymen (membrane) plus pteron (wing). The way we were taught about our hymens – as a barrier that would inevitably be breached – meant I visualised it as something thick and tough, bubblegum pink, that would pop when broken.

*

On holiday in Turkey, at breakfast, we sat down at a table beside a low brick wall upon which had been placed a small white plate.

The inner circle of the plate was dotted with pieces of sausage, red and chopped into small chunks.

Beyond the plate was a bed of rosemary, then olive trees, flits of small brown birds, then the flat expanse of the Aegean sea.

The purpose of the plate was to act as a distraction for the wasps, who otherwise bothered the guests throughout their morning meal.

The bait was working – the plate playing host to between five and ten wasps at any given moment.

The plate was a source of constant movement in my peripheral vision, the bodies of the wasps catching the light, treading over the meat, occasionally taking flight to hover and land again.

The amount of sausage diminished through the course of breakfast as the wasps filled with meat.

The perimeter of a trampoline is covered with a hem of blue plastic. This plastic covers the rim of large, tight springs, which allow the netting to give.

When setting up the beds at the start of practice and dismantling them at the end, the person leading would shout 'Watch your fingers!' as the trampoline snapped open into place and again, 'Fingers!' when it chomped closed like a huge mouth. The springs were totally rigid. Like pipes. I would sometimes touch them underneath the blue rim and smell the metal on my hands.

At one competition which looked like all other competitions – a large yellow hall with very high ceilings and brick walls painted white, no windows – a girl crashed on the blue. One leg slipped under the plastic and became stuck between the springs right up to the very top of her thigh. I recall only that her scream was brief and very loud and rang out like a bell.

*

I remember my neighbour, a girl the same age as me, saying to me in the back seat of a car as we shared a lift into training, 'Sometimes I pretend I'm listening to what you're saying but I'm just thinking I want to pull your eyelashes out.' Her honesty impressed me.

*

Vending machines, dim beige halls used for badminton and football, the brightly coloured tape that marked out the courts on the varnished floor begging to be picked at, strip lights, carpeted stairs, bottles of frozen orange squash, blackcurrant squash, an expanse of blue plastic and cream mesh.

Motorways, generic hotels, rain on windows as jewels, four to a room. I knew Birmingham only by its arena, Cardiff by the high-up windows above the judges' table, Guildford by the tuck shop by the toilets.

Neece French plaiting my hair as I sit on the floor in front of her.

The lights in hotel rooms: red dot on TV; blue dot on TV; slice coming from under the bathroom door, pushed to; sliver between the curtains; digital alarm clock, blinking; line underneath the room's door, from the hall, which leads to the fire exit at one end, memorised in the event of smoke from fire. A constellation around mum, dad, brother, sleeping. A map to memorise in the event of waking, needing reassurance that you are not dead.

At this point I was competing regularly, scores from national competitions being recorded by a faceless governing body who would one day call one of my coaches and inform them that my average score was one of the four top scores for the season, and therefore made me eligible for a place at the World Age Group Games in Canada. The same was true for James and Scott, and our older club-mate, Jane.

The tracksuit was expensive and a bit too big. I tried it on in the homes of various relatives – blue trousers and a red and white jacket.

In the second VHS I am ten years old, competing at the World Age Group Games. I am in the back corner of a large sports stadium. The video must have been taken by one of my parents or my brother, with his predilection for gadgets. My coach is down on the stadium floor with me, by the side of the trampoline. By that age I would have been strong enough to raise myself onto the trampoline without assistance, using the metal bars underneath the blue rim as a foothold, but it's possible that, given the magnitude of the occasion, my coach would have lifted me up and placed me on the edge.

The work of the entire previous season, and really my entire career to date, had brought us to this point. I complete the first eight moves of the routine and then, dangerously close to the crash mat, improvise two moves which propel me back towards the cross. It was a move smart enough that I didn't score for an incomplete routine or have marks deducted for hitting the mat. To do those things would have been utter disaster.

But it wasn't the routine I had registered. You pledge a performance and you must deliver it.

I land in the vast safe space between total failure and absolute perfection. It seems I am an expert at dropping the reins at the last minute.

We had travelled all that way for those ten moves.

I finish the routine and instantly burst into tears. On the video my arms are held straight out in front of me for two or three seconds to prove balance, and I am crying as I salute the judges. I placed eleventh in the world.

When I found my old scrapbook from the trip, I saw that I had recorded Sophie and I placing fourth in the world in the synchronised category, a fact I had completely forgotten. My parents have since mentioned that Sophie made a mistake which meant we didn't get a podium position – I have no memory of it.

It occurs to me now that amid the fear there was so much joy in it too.

On a Friday night after training our parents would go to the leisure centre bar for a drink. Often we would pile into a huge room above the hall we trained in which was set out for martial arts. We would wrestle and tumble until we were told it was time to leave, or until, finally tired, we filed down to the bar. In breaks at training sessions, or in the slow hours at competitions, we would often find a grassy patch nearby and practice somersaulting on the spot, or backflips, or walking on our hands.

We spent three weeks in Canada. Two of them travelling Banff and Toronto, making the trip worthwhile, and the final one confined to a sports stadium. My family stayed in a hotel and I spent my time with the squad in a large dormitory, bunk beds tessellated in a large, oddly shaped room. When we arrived the squad members who were already there had been having a water balloon fight. The front steps were strewn with brightly coloured scraps of plastic. I don't think I had fully comprehended that I would be staying there alone. James and Scott were upstairs in the boys' dormitory and Jane must have been in a different section of the room with the older girls. The four of us in the under-11 category slept in two bunkbeds in a nook close to the door. I would look at the outlines of the girls in their beds, in what I recall was a cool navy light, as I tried to get to sleep.

In Banff I remember I felt happy. I stood on a large glacier wearing denim cut-offs and a sweatshirt. It wasn't even slippery. It glittered.

*

In my scrapbook, on the final page underneath the title 'My Favourite Photo', is a picture of me and Jane standing on the iceberg, clutching one another, beaming.

To the side of the photo I have written 'Me and Jane on an iceberg. It was very, very slippery'.

*

After Canada, Sophie's coach broke our coupling so that she could team up with one of her clubmates instead.

I believe this was perceived as something of an insult following our success together, and my very marginal superiority as an athlete, but I don't recall that I minded or really had feelings about it one way or the other.

I was paired with a new partner, ranked lower than me but far superior in style. Considerably more brave. The one I feared. The one I held back.

We began training together regularly. My parents or coach would drive me an hour or so to their larger, much better equipped club. Sometimes a few of us would go as a group to use their facilities; trampolines permanently set out in a huge blue and white sea, a tumbling strip that ran the length of the huge hall, two large pits filled with foam bricks into which you could launch yourself and land on practically any part of your body without worrying. I couldn't quite believe the trampolines stayed out permanently, that the hall was used for our sport and our sport alone. I imagined them at night, resting in the dark hall.

*

When I was twelve, a sharp pain shot up my lower back when my feet hit the trampoline. Once it arrived, it stayed. Falling into pain is a strange feeling. Jumping away from it, knowing it is coming again very soon. Choosing the pain, being helpless to stop it.

I started wearing a back support. It was beige, second-hand, and wrapped around my torso with parallel velcro strips. It worked basically like a corset, squeezing the pain. Between routines a fellow trampolinist or a coach would rewrap me.

Deep Heat was ever-present at training sessions – the smell of it pricking the air. People with their special little area – a shoulder or a thigh – that needed anointing.

I kept training, wincing, took time off to rest. Began to fall behind. My coach mentioned the new moves I was expected to learn before the start of the new season, that a failure to do so would set me back, see me snapping at the heels of my peers. It was the first time I realised my future came with certain expectations, a schedule, that my trajectory could see me spinning out into a galaxy of double somersaults, triple somersaults, moves that it scared me to watch other people performing.

Towards the end of my career I was told, minutes before I was due to perform a synchronised routine, that I couldn't compete with such a visible injury. The man who made this decision and delivered the news routinely marked me lower at competitions than the other judges. My mum had decided long ago that he had something against me. I remember his full name, his face, his hairline, a good approximation of his height and size. I could make a little doll of him.

The support wouldn't fit under my leotard. I unwrapped myself and fell into the inevitable, open and searing.

Language in art remains a highly ambiguous transaction, a quicksand, a trampoline, a frozen pool which might give way under you… at any time.
—Harold Pinter

My white trampolining shoes are in a box under my bed with other things I can hardly bear to look at but can't throw away. Markers of a different life and time – how quickly it is passing.

I have a birthday card from Neece from about a month before she died, given to me on my 25th birthday. She handed it to me from her wheelchair on a tram platform in Croydon. She had fallen asleep at the table after eating the cake. James gently roused her.

Months before, her spine had been reconstructed with metal rods. I saw the scan. The white poles set up like scaffolding.

When we were called and told she was dying – had been sedated and now wouldn't wake up – I was by chance at my mum and dad's, sleeping in my old single bed. I called my dad, who was out, and struggled to speak the words.

We sat around her bed in a yellow hospital room. Scott arrived after us, immediately took her hand out from underneath the neat white sheet and held it as if she were still alive, which she was. We surrounded her bed and talked about the life we had all shared together.

We went home, had dinner. I stood opposite my brother in our family kitchen and said I didn't want to go back to the hospital the next morning. My brother said it wasn't anything to be afraid of and he meant it. I felt very ashamed of my desire to run from the situation, of how sick death made me feel.

We were told it would be a couple more days but she died that night, with her husband asleep in the chair beside her, as if she would prefer it be done quickly and with no one watching.

The following day, we had all gathered at her house. My family and hers squeezed on to the sofas and drank cans of beer through the afternoon. I was horrified by my relief that I would never again have to watch her dying.

At a house party when I was around twenty-five, a friend knocked over and smashed a vase she had given me when I moved out of my family home. When everyone left, I stood at the door crying, drunk, in the middle of the night, as my boyfriend tried to retrieve the shards from the bin. It was hopeless. So many pieces unaccounted for or swept away.

*

The main hall I trained in was set up with four trampolines in a grid, with no spaces between them. A curtain, running the width of the hall and weighted at the bottom, could be pulled from one side to the other in order to separate us from the rest of the activity in the hall. The top third of the curtain was mesh – at the height of a jump you could see shuttlecocks flying over the net.

The hall had a viewing window for spectators – probably only three metres by two metres – placed in an odd little room next to the café. There were a couple of chairs (and a table?) in front of the window. When I imagine looking up at the window from the hall I see my mum sitting with my brother, or chatting to another parent, or a coach. When I was smaller I used to enjoy watching the older children training through the glass. The café itself was lined with three squash courts in which my dad would often play on a Saturday. I would get a Slush Puppie on a break and watch him for a minute, loving the crack of the ball hitting the wall of the court, the echo.

Occasionally, after practice, we could get something from the vending machine. Smoky bacon Wheat Crunchies, Rib n' Saucy Nik Naks, Caramac bars and, my favourite, a Secret bar in its white paper case. There was such joy in the selection of the item you wanted, the pressing of the correct letter and number combination, watching as the metal twisted and it fell.

I often fantasised that I would halt at the very highest point in a jump and hover there, then begin to circle the perimeter of the sports hall looking down on the array of beds with their red crosses and select which one to descend to, very slowly.

Friends used to ask me if trampolining felt like flying to which I replied that it did, knowing it was the answer they wanted.

When I sit alone in my garden now, I track the journeys of individual bees. Snapdragon – dahlia – verbena – salvia – dandelion – sedum – broad bean flowers – cosmos – cosmos – cosmos – willing them to settle.

In my early 30s, sitting on a bench in the walled garden attached to All Hallows Church, my reading was interrupted by my benchfellow saying, 'I'm sorry but you have a...' and pointing to the exposed skin of my ankle, upon which rested a dragonfly, gleaming in the early spring sun.

We both observed the creature – which was really incredibly beautiful – for a few seconds, and he returned to the lunch he was eating from a tupperware with a fork.

Needless to say I hadn't felt the dragonfly land on my ankle and, even then, I could feel nothing, though I willed myself to. The dragonfly stayed very still, seeming dead, and didn't fly away even when, after many minutes, I crossed my ankle on the opposite knee and blew on it gently.

I stayed on the bench for longer than I had intended, allowing it to be where it wanted, wondering if I should interpret it as a sign.

I knew very little about dragonflies. I discovered that they spend most of their lives as nymphs on the water, and a matter of weeks or days on the wing. In its bodily metamorphosis, a dragonfly carries its nymph brain into its new form.

When I close my eyes I can also inhabit my younger body with ease; I remember the feeling of my nose touching my knees when I stretched before training. I recall the weight of a gymnastics coach, hard hands on my back pushing me down into splits. I have physical recollection of every move I ever knew how to do.

In the months following the incident with the dragonfly, I sensed it was becoming bluer with each remembering. I developed a wish to have touched it with a finger and question what it wanted, though I'd had no such compulsion at the time. It had been stubborn, like a grief that wouldn't break. Perhaps it was simply presenting itself.

*

At the last National Finals competition I took part in, the top 10 was decided on the first day of competition.

That 10 would compete for a second time – repeating their voluntary routine – the next day.

I had placed eighth on day one.

I sensed from people outside of my team and family that this was a disappointing showing from the girl who was allegedly eleventh best in the world.

I must have overheard something, or perhaps someone was bold enough to say so.

In the evening, the sports hall was dark, lit with flashing lights, and loud music played. I remember being delighted, going to sleep that night, that the worst thing that could happen the next day would be to place tenth, even if I fell off without completing a single move. What a relief for there to be a limit to failure.

*

I have no memory of how I managed my periods during competitions, when no clothing is allowed besides the leotard in its infallible and total purity. As a trampolinist you become an expert at pulling your leotard aside to urinate, running and returning in record time just before your turn to compete.

Very quickly after my periods began at the age of 12 I developed an irrational – or arguably absolutely rational – fear of inserting tampons and can't recall that I ever used one for the purposes of competing.

One afternoon, probably in the late 1990s, I saw an open newspaper on the kitchen counter. The newspaper reported on the intensive regime of a famous Russian gymnast which, retrospectively, seemed to imply a level of cruelty had been exercised that we would never allow at home. A result of this regime was that the gymnast – pictured in pose on the beam, arms extended behind her head, rib cage protruding, lower back very curved – had ceased to have periods. She had been pushed too far.

*

In my early twenties, after a decade of infrequent and unremarkable internal examinations, there was an incident with a bad gynaecologist. After that incident I became very protective of my body, specifically the space between my navel and the top of my pubic hair.

Protective like I wanted to shield it with my hands or separate it from my body and wrap it in soft cloth like an injured animal.

During the first part of the inspection with the bad gynaecologist, as a feeling of uneasiness began to creep over me, I tried to distract myself by looking at the fuzzy black and white footage of my uterus on the small screen to my right.

Looking inside yourself and willing your brain to make sense of it is asking too much.

The mysterious and private dark – something you have only ever sensed – suddenly framed in front of you.

If an astronaut had one word for the feeling of observing the whole of the earth from space, as did a human viewing their insides on a screen, I think that word would be: no.

I didn't know until years after my retirement, at the age of fifteen, that trampolines were initially conceived as a means of preparing astronauts for the bodily experiences of being in space.

Training for acceleration and spinning and the art of control when there is nothing to hold on to.

In trampolining it takes time, when you've learnt a new move, for your brain, eyes, ears, limbs to understand what is happening to your body and accept it.

After years of performing tens of somersaults in a row you can land, pause, walk to the edge of the bed and dismount without so much as a wobble. Your body calibrates as it goes along, carries on as if nothing has happened or as if you simply took a step.

But when you learn something new, your body knows this is new territory. Your eyes lag by a second or two and your balance fails.

The bad gynaecologist looked intently at his computer screen as my body began the process of losing consciousness. I was now dressed and sitting back beside his desk wearing a complimentary sanitary towel in anticipation of the bleeding I presumed would come, pain of that kind not seeming possible without the logical accompaniment of blood.

There was a time when the existence of periods was used as an argument to stop astronauts who experienced menstrual bleeding from going into space.

It was known that being in space can cause muscle atrophy and deterioration of the skeleton, slowing of cardiovascular system functions, decreased production of red blood cells, and balance and eyesight disorders.

Why not then the flowing of blood back into the body? Or the floating of blood out into the atmosphere, uncontained?

The window above the bad gynaecologist's desk was rectangular. Very wide but short, like an arrow slit on its side. Except not at all, or no more than his pen was a sword and the silver door handle an arrow. All morphing into a collection of objects for inflicting injury, into a narrative of violence. I hated him.

The bad gynaecologist clicked the mouse, tapped a key – the room was turning white – as he pretended I didn't exist.

*

Sometimes at training I looked at the girl who had smashed her face into her knee and tried to imagine the plate underneath her skin. When it had happened people kept stating the number of screws and pins she had in addition to the plate. Was it 12 screws? Five pins? Could she feel them in her face when she talked, when she smiled? Did she think of them when she washed her face or applied make up?

She stopped trampolining at some point – either losing interest or because she couldn't keep up – and I wondered if she felt it had been worth it.

*

I was afraid of one of my coaches. She didn't tolerate my nervousness and had no time for excuses. She was serious, though she had a generally mischievous disposition and laughed a lot. I suppose she was serious about trampolining. Looking back I think she wanted to make me strong. I wanted to impress her at the same time as I wished she would disappear from my life.

At one session, probably around nine years old, I was in the process of learning a new move – a 'rudi' – straight front somersault with one and a half twists. A really beautiful move, like a Twister lolly. After some time – having executed a straight front somersault with one full twist safely, repeatedly – she said that I should twist slightly earlier. For some reason I was reluctant to complete the new move that day, although I was so close. I checked that I wouldn't be doing the full move and she reassured me. She said to twist when she shouted 'Now!'. I followed her command and of course, momentum being what it is, I completed the full one and a half twist, landing perfectly and cleanly on the crash mat.

She had tricked me, thinking for my own good, but I felt embarrassed, like a puppet. But worse, no one was even manipulating the strings – I had done it all on my own. She possessed my body with a single word. It was shocking.

When I was told she wasn't due at a session I didn't believe it and looked at the door of the sports hall constantly throughout the session, waiting for her to manifest like a ghost at the strike of midnight.

*

It hit me one day, perhaps the girl in the story was turned to glass and not stone?

Perhaps everything was turned to glass but maintained its colour – transparent green apples hanging from the tree, her glass bones visible through her glass skin and clothes and that the greyness of the scene was my imagining.

*

I don't remember the first time it happened but suddenly, one day, I was leaking. The impact of landing on the trampoline forcing a tiny bit of liquid into my underwear. To begin with it must have been manageable, or infrequent, but before too long I was wearing a sanitary towel to train. I would limit the amount I was drinking during training and run to the toilet before my turn, almost every time, to force out anything that might be stored inside. But nothing worked – it kept coming, I didn't know from where, and filling the pads multiple times a session.

I became completely preoccupied with whether this was visible to anyone else, what colour shorts or tracksuit bottoms to wear. Before I landed each jump, my mind was not on the move coming next, but how much would come out.

I was lucky to have a relationship with my mum in which I could be very open about my body and its changes. I told her and she told my coach. The three of us knew, and that felt better, but I told no one else, not even my school friends with whom I shared everything. As with my periods, I don't remember how I managed this in competitions.

My body felt out of my control and it was embarrassing me.

All my life, when I have retold the story of my retirement, I have omitted this detail, focusing instead on my injuries or my ineptitude for competition.

Fear of devils, death, that they shall be so sick, of some such or such disease, ready to tremble at every object, they shall die themselves forthwith… that they are all glass, and therefore will suffer no man to come near them; that they are all cork, as light as feathers; others as heavy as lead; some are afraid their heads will fall off their shoulders, that they have frogs in their bellies, Etc.
—The Anatomy of Melancholy by Robert Burton, 1621

As I got older, into my early teens, my fears – about what I couldn't control with regard to my body, my perception of my brain as the saboteur at the helm of my body – became more severe.

Learning a double back somersault requires considerable height and, once I was out of the rig and practising using only the crash mat, I once reached the top of the jump and realised that my brain could do anything it wanted to me. I remember this realisation hitting me so suddenly.

I added to the fear of throwing myself in the wrong direction or leaping off the trampoline sideways – which only happened to me once, and with minimal consequences – a fear of my neck snapping backwards, a fear of my teeth snapping closed and biting off my tongue, of the tendons in my legs snapping. What did my body contain that couldn't snap? The more I thought about it, quite literally nothing.

Trampolining textbooks list the below as possible injuries associated with the sport:

- Cuts, grazes
- Bruises
- Bitten tongue
- Nose bleed
- Ankle injuries
- Knee injuries
- Wrist and forearm
- Head injury
- Spinal injury
- Broken limb bone

I cannot recall that I ever witnessed a nose bleed.

—

At a point, my dreams about my teeth became so constant and graphic that I was able to talk to myself within my dream, making assurances that, though my teeth might be loosening and falling, or growing rapidly from both rows to such a length that I resembled a mutant rat before they snapped into pieces, I was very much in my bed asleep, all my teeth quiet in my head.

—

Glass delusion – the belief that your body, or a part of it, is made of glass and could shatter at any moment – was first recorded in the Middle Ages and eventually became a not-uncommon malady among royals and nobles in the Middle Ages, before becoming virtually unheard of by the end of the 1800s. King Charles VI of France, having ascended to the throne age 11, had spells during which he believed his entire body to be made from glass and would lie motionless wrapped in layers of blankets, only moving when wearing a special protective garment complete with metal ribs.

*

The idea of the girl being made of glass was only a half thought. I created it so that my memory might be jolted by indignance – compelled to correct it. But I knew it was stone. And wherever she had sat, she remained.

*

A discussion of competitive anxiety requires the establishment of a common language that allows precise and efficient communication… When studying a social science, students must frequently learn new meanings to words they already know, giving these familiar terms precise meanings to describe specific phenomena. Anxiety, stress, arousal, and competition are terms familiar to all of us, but scientific rigor requires that precise definitions for these complex phenomena replace the vague, general meanings that these words have in our everyday vocabularies.

—Competitive Anxiety in Sport by Damon Burton, Rainer Martens, and Robin S. Vealey, 1990

Glossary of competitive anxiety terms:

State anxiety
One morning, having stayed at my grandparent's flat for the night, my brother and I woke to discover that an infection had glued his eyes shut during the night. The skin of his eyelids stretched with the effort to open them, my baby mole brother, trying to come into the light. I soaked some tissue in milk and dabbed it on his eyes. Slowly, small gaps appeared beneath his eyelashes as the two lids became unstuck.

Trait anxiety

I remember, on those nights we stayed over and I lay awake in terror, the tiny movements of the net curtains, illuminated by the moon and streetlights.

Cognitive anxiety

Me and my brother were very different children who both, in phases, had small facial tics that our parents gently tried to police out of existence.

Threat

I liked to pull down the sleeves of my leotard until they covered my hands completely. I liked to zip up my tracksuit top right to the chin.

Somatic anxiety

Trampolining is complete exposure: just your body, the air around it, rotation, momentum – too much or not enough – red cross, red cross, red cross.

Arousal

At competitions, I could never recreate the feeling I had when I trampolined at a club training session, in the familiar hall, on the beds I knew. Elsewhere, I felt removed from my body, floating around myself. Like I couldn't locate my brain, in my body, in the air.

Stress

When my dad came in to say goodnight, he would say, 'Night night, god bless' a couple of times as he walked to the door and as he shut it. I would say back, 'Night night, god bless' once or twice so that he could hear, but always a total of five times after the door closed. As he walked down the stairs, I would count 9, 10, 11, 12 in my head, five times.

*

I remember a period of prolonged unhappiness and fear. A few of us trained twice a week in a different hall, away from the majority of the club. The hall was unfamiliar, too bright, cold. It exists in my memory as a white cube with court markings across the floor in red tape.

I decided I wanted to stop.

I started to cry at a training session on a Monday night. I remember no details besides sitting on a bench in a changing room I'd never been in before, telling the coach who scared me that I didn't want to, couldn't, do it any more. She was very kind.

There was a sanitary towel in its purple wrapper on the floor of the room.

She understood. She said *Stop. It's supposed to be fun for you.* My parents said *Of course, it's fine, stop.*

I didn't go to training sessions for a matter of weeks before changing my mind, I suppose missing it, feeling I had been a quitter, thrown all those years away. I have never had a huge amount of belief in the decisions I make. I wonder if anyone does.

I returned to training. I like to think that a part of me missed being in the air.

I am waiting for the delayed collapse of my body. A crumbling of joints and wearing of cartilage. I think of it like a shattered but still-standing window.

Both of my lower ribs pop on a regular basis. I hate the sensation. This happens when the lower ribs, attached to the rest of the cage only by cartilage, come slightly loose, usually because of impact or trauma. Who knows if this would have happened anyway.

My hips sometimes hurt, as do my shoulders from years of over-extension and the bone grinding into the socket like a pestle into a mortar. My back injury sometimes flares up as I walk – a white-hot pain out of nowhere making me stop dead in the street – and disappears as quickly as it came.

In my first job after university I worked as an editorial assistant at a publisher of pharmaceutical textbooks. Among the books I edited were titles dedicated to zoonoses, pharmacokinetics, an A-Z of diseases. A book which suggested that the best way to combat fear of death was to dedicate some time to think about it each day, which for a while I did, to no effect. But the one I recall best, and yet can't recall the exact content of, featured a section which attempted to define pain. The attempt was so abstract that, had I not known the subject of those pages, I don't think I would ever have guessed it.

*

During the 2012 London Olympics I watched my former synchronised trampolining partner, now an adult, compete for Great Britain. I had messaged her before the Games started to wish her good luck. We told each other, briefly, about our lives.

I watched her on my laptop, holding my breath, instantly knowing her style, willing her to get to the end of her routine, wondering how did she do it, how did she push through.

*

Eventually someone else located the girl for me. They messaged and said they thought they had found the story I was looking for, which bore many resemblances, other than that the girl did not turn to stone.

I was doubtful.

But as soon as I saw the title, *The Black Bull of Norroway*, I knew it was the one. I read one version, then another, searching for the variation I was so sure existed.

> *For a long time they rode and rode, until they came to a barren and brooding glen. The girl slid off the bull's back and sat down on a stone.*

> *They rode, and they rode, and they rode, till they came to a dark and ugsome glen. And here he bade her dismount and sit on a great rock.*

> *And aye they rode, and on they rode, till they came to a dark and ugsome glen, where they stopped, and the lady lighted down. Says the Bull to her: "Here you must stay till I go and fight the Old One. You must seat yourself on that stone, and move neither hand nor foot till I come back.*

There was no tree trunk sat upon, but a stone.

> So the girl sat, moving not even her eyes, until all about her turned blue. Overjoyed by the bull's triumph, she shifted where she sat. So when the bull returned to look for her he could not find her.

> Well, she sate as still as a mouse, moving neither hand nor foot, nor even her eyes, and waited, and waited, and waited. Then at last everything turned blue. But she was so overcome with joy to think that her lover was victorious that she forgot to keep still, and lifting one of her feet, crossed it over the other! So she waited, and waited, and waited. Long she sate, and aye she wearied; and all the time he was seeking for her, but he never found her.

> She set herself down on the stone, and by-and-by all around her turned blue. Overcome with joy, she lifted one of her feet, and crossed it over the other, so glad was she that her companion was victorious. The Bull returned and sought for her, but never could find her.

No tree trunk. A stone. No petrification, but the bull unable to locate her. I had supplanted an invisible girl with a stone girl, a stone with a tree trunk.

Before this, they had ridden together for days, with the girl eating from the bull's right ear and drinking from his left.

The point at which the bull wins his duel, the sky flashes blue, the girl moves a foot and cannot be found again – all this occurs a third of the way into the story. Then follows the girl's quest to find the bull, her love (it turns out, a prince bewitched): a hill made of glass the girl cannot climb, seven years of servitude in return for iron shoes with which to climb it. Locating the bull, now a man, and betrothed to be married – a successful postponement of the wedding and eventual happiness.

I had cut her life off at the point of failure.

*

I wasn't the best; I was relatively fast. I trained, ate, travelled, and showered with the best in the country, but wasn't the best; I was pretty good.
—*Swimming Studies* by Leanne Shapton

When, as an adult, I read Leanne Shapton's account of her years as a competitive swimmer, I shared almost every feeling she recounted. How many of us, I wondered, had been very good but not the best? The space between the two is immeasurable.

But, even now, with it all behind her, her need to be in water seems compulsive. It is her element.

Air was not mine.

Yet, in my dreams, when I am trying to escape danger I move down the street in huge somersaults, over fences, over water. I never run.

Another recurring dream involves me being taken to my old leisure centre, the age I am now, and instructed to perform the same routine from the World Age Group Games. There is always an element of peril – a threat to my life or that of my

91

family. I have never stayed in the dream long enough to find out if I'm successful, but I think about it a lot. I still believe the moves are somewhere in there. A part of me thinks I could do it.

After Neece died, she appeared in my dreams regularly, alive and healthy. I was always pleased to see her in sleep, and pleased when I woke up. She appears now, still, but rarely. I am grateful that she visits me kindly in my dreams, which never feel like a haunting, though I know other people who have been tormented by the appearances of their dearly departed, waking to confront the loss all over again.

*

I wonder why I was so quick to dismiss air as my element. I existed in it for years, as naturally as I walked and breathed. Thrived in it, even.

Now, I love to swim. For a while I took this to be an interesting development – was I reaching out for the opposite sensation to being in the air? Rejecting all those years of exposure by immersing myself in water? But of course there's nothing interesting about it – to swim and to fly are both to inhabit the completely untethered body.

I think again about the dragonfly's shell of a body, like a paper-thin bone. The sound it would make if carried by a breeze across a hard surface.

It became bluer and bluer in my memory.

*

E ven my fabricated memory – that of the girl being turned to glass – was closer to the truth of the story. Except a hill, not the girl, is glass, and appears in the very next paragraph.

> After this she felt heartened up, and wandered on till her
> road was blocked by a great hill of glass; and though she
> tried all she could to climb it, she could not; for aye she
> slipped back, and slipped back, and slipped back; for it was
> like ice.

> She walked and walked until she came to a hill of glass. Try
> as she might, she could not climb it for its slopes were sheer
> and slippery.

> On she wandered, till she came to a great hill of glass, that
> she tried all she could to climb, but wasn't able.

*

My ultimate extrication from competition and training is something I remember nothing about. I can't recall making the decision once and for all, how long it came after my first attempt to leave. I don't remember a single conversation I had, my last training session, or competition. I don't know who told my coaches, or my synchronised partner, or how anyone responded. It's a shocking blank.

Did the trophies remain on display under the stairs? Were my drawers still full of leotards and white socks? What did we do with all the hours we gained? Did I thank my coaches for the years of time and care they put into me? Did I thank my parents, my brother? Did I apologise?

*

In the years following my retirement, I would go to my old club to bounce casually. I enjoyed throwing myself around, free from the constraints of training or expectation. One of the last times I went, I lost a move. The barani – a simple front somersault with a half twist – is the first twisting somersault you learn. It's easy and had always been one of my favourite moves to play around with, sometimes doing 10 or 20 in a row, bouncing back and forth like a pinball.

I went back again a few weeks later to try and get it back. Rob went into coach mode, breaking the move down into its component parts – a front somersault with a decisive kick out, then a front somersault with a decisive kick out followed by the half twist. One move, two motions, over and over until it becomes one motion again. But it didn't click. It didn't come back. I gave up trying.

I have no idea now, if I tried again, whether it would be waiting there in my pocket ready to be retrieved, or floating out in deep space, way beyond my reach.

*

When I watch videos of trampolinists online, I remember all of the small movements we relied on to gain height, to find our balance in the air, to travel forwards or backwards. Tiny adjustments: a bending of a leg, one arm at a slight angle, like a plane finding its line of flight after take-off.

When I watch these videos I can sense when the routine is going to begin. The athlete's body changes, as if the air is flowing through it.

Sometimes I will close my eyes and listen to the sound of bed creaking, the air rushing through the mesh, the reverberation as the body connects with the bed. A friend, after watching a video I sent, said, 'The noise the trampoline makes! The shudder.'

*

I like it when memories aren't pinned haughtily to words.
—*Hawthorn* by Zaffar Kunial

A series of images:

Sitting on a bench in a sports hall. James on the bench in the row below me. He turns around and picks something from my hair.

Landing the final move of a routine, looking to my left and seeing Scott on the trampoline next to me, holding the same position, grinning back at me.

Watching James, in the rig, attempting a triple back somersault, falling 180 degrees short.

A very hot day, the light hitting the floor of the training hall through an open fire escape.

My brother playing a Game Boy in the back of the car, in the seat beside me.

On my front on a trampoline, looking through the mesh at someone lying on the floor below me.

Canoeing on Lake Louise in Canada after the Games were over. The bright orange of the life jacket on the person in front of me – the unbelievably vivid, milky blue water. A blue that has been verified by photographs.

My mum and dad in the stalls of a stadium – dad's eyes moving up and down as he watched someone bounce, mum looking down, reaching into a backpack.

A line of judges behind a white table, revealing their scores in relative unison – red numbers on white cards.

Opening the freezer drawer and retrieving a bloated bottle of frozen water.

Rob, both hands on a crash mat at the edge of a trampoline, his body bobbing up and down to keep time with the person on the bed.

Neece with her face in her hands, unable to watch as one of her sons competes.

*

When I swim now I step into the water as though
absentmindedly touching a scar.
—*Swimming Studies* by Leanne Shapton

At the age of twenty-seven I got on a trampoline again. A group
of us sat in a café by the side of the lake, drinking beer. Me and
James, our lives forever intertwined, decided to bounce.

He had continued to train and compete into his early twenties
and even on a small, meshed trampoline designed for children,
he was stunning.

I was in the early stages of drunkenness and wearing a long
black sundress.

I limited myself to the handful of moves – mostly simple
somersaults – that I'd done so many thousands of times I didn't
even need to think. A group of children gathered to watch us.
I did one move, a lazy back – a straight backwards somersault
landing in a front drop – many times. The motion of it is very
pleasing and mimics the way a cherub might come to rest on a
cloud.

I was warned many times, before puberty came, that once my

breasts grew it would start to hurt to land on my front. It never did.

I was fascinated by Jane's breasts, which jolted down sharply when she landed on the bed.

Afterwards we sat back down, slightly out of breath. My little cousin came over and stood beside me, told me to stay very still. I did as instructed, tilted my head back and he placed a small plastic bug on my nose.

I focused on the toy's many bent legs, its black, painted eyes. It balanced there. My cousin was delighted. He removed the bug.

The mesh had felt warm and safe on my bare feet. Being upside down, in the air, was completely usual. I hope it will always feel that way.

Nothing was ripped apart. My feet tingled with the memory of it. It felt like old knowledge.

Also available from Makina Books

In **Strangers**, Rebecca Tamás explores where the human and nonhuman meet, and why this delicate connection just might be the most important relationship of our times. From 'On Watermelon' to 'On Grief', Tamás' essays are exhilarating to read in their radical and original exploration of the links between the environmental, the political, the folkloric and the historical.

Dust Sucker is a remarkable new book-length poem by writer and translator Jen Calleja. Clear-eyed, expansive, and intoxicating, this exhilarating work deftly blurs disparate themes including time and mortality, communication and translation, intimacy and infertility.

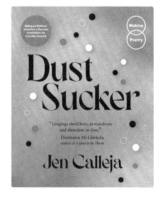

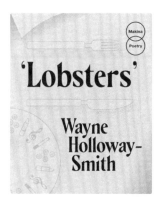

In **Lobsters**, Wayne Holloway-Smith turns his innovative poetics towards an exhilarating new work that is part songbook, part elastic melodrama. Somewhere, in between the expansive and claustrophobic, the reader is offered a new space, crammed full with the music of what life gives and withholds.

Hyperlove burns with frustration and fervour. In this incisive lyric essay, the creative mixes with the critical, as Morris looks to the mystics, to pop culture, to writing itself, dislocating categories of love and forming a radical and original exploration of desire as a woman.

Makina Books are an independent publisher based in London. Our publications, audio and audio-described projects seek to promote and celebrate independent and emerging voices—with a particular focus on poetry and nonfiction.

For more information on our forthcoming titles and projects please visit us at **makinabooks.com**